SCIENCE AND TECHNOLOGY START-UP STARS

MEDICAL Entrepreneurs

Helen Mason

CRABTREE
PUBLISHING COMPANY
WWW.CRABTREEBOOKS.COM

CRABTREE
PUBLISHING COMPANY
WWW.CRABTREEBOOKS.COM

Author: Helen Mason

Editors: Sarah Eason, Nancy Dickmann, Wendy Scavuzzo, and Petrice Custance

Proofreader and indexer: Wendy Scavuzzo

Editorial director: Kathy Middleton

Design: Clare Webber

Cover design and additional artwork: Clare Webber

Photo research: Rachel Blount

Production coordinator and Prepress technician: Tammy McGarr

Print coordinator: Katherine Berti

Consultant: David Hawksett

Produced for Crabtree Publishing Company by Calcium Creative

Photo Credits:

t=Top, tr=Top Right, tl=Top Left

Inside: CoachmePlus: p. 11t; Flickr: RIC: p. 15t; Kinnos Inc.: p. 27;

Easton LaChappelle: pp. 3, 4, 16c, 16b; Mobius Bionics: Photo courtesy Mobius Bionics LLC. Used with permission: p. 14; Neopenda: pp. 24, 25t, 25b; Psyonic: p. 15b; Shutterstock: Andrey Popov: p. 22; Aspen Photo:
p. 11b; Christoph Burgstedt: pp. 1, 26; CI Photos: p. 6; Click and Photo: p. 23t; CNK02: p. 5b; Designua: p. 18r; FamVeld: p. 23b; Komsan Loonprom: p. 20; Mehendra_art: p. 5t; Zaharia Bogdan Rares: p. 10; Science Photo: p. 28; Ververidis Vasilis: p. 29; Jovan Vitanovski: p. 8; WitthayaP: p. 9; Sparta Science: p. 12t; Tutublue: p. 7; Wikimedia Commons: Nissim Benvenisty: p. 19; Đ℮: p. 21; Evan-Amos: p. 17; Ryan Knapp: p. 13; Thomson200: p. 12b; The U.S. Food and Drug Administration: p. 18l; Wellcome Images: p. 5r.

Cover: Shutterstock: Ash T Productions.

Library and Archives Canada Cataloguing in Publication

Mason, Helen, 1950-, author
     Medical entrepreneurs / Helen Mason.

(Science and technology start-up stars)
Includes index.
Issued in print and electronic formats.
ISBN 978-0-7787-4421-4 (hardcover).--
ISBN 978-0-7787-4434-4 (softcover).--
ISBN 978-1-4271-2025-0 (HTML)

    1. Medical innovations--Juvenile literature. 2. Medical care--Technological innovations--Juvenile literature. 3. Medical technology--Juvenile literature. 4. Entrepreneurship--Juvenile literature. I. Title.

RA418.5.M4M37 2018   j610   C2017-907703-1
                                      C2017-907704-X

Library of Congress Cataloging-in-Publication Data

CIP available at the Library of Congress

Crabtree Publishing Company

www.crabtreebooks.com   1-800-387-7650

Printed in the U.S.A./022018/CG20171220

Published in Canada
Crabtree Publishing
616 Welland Ave.
St. Catharines, Ontario
L2M 5V6

Published in the United States
Crabtree Publishing
PMB 59051
350 Fifth Avenue, 59th Floor
New York, New York 10118

Published in the United Kingdom
Crabtree Publishing
Maritime House
Basin Road North, Hove
BN41 1WR

Published in Australia
Crabtree Publishing
3 Charles Street
Coburg North
VIC, 3058

CONTENTS

YOU CAN BE AN ENTREPRENEUR!

In July 2017, 21-year-old **entrepreneur** Easton LaChappelle printed a **prosthetic** arm on a **3-D printer**. He presented the arm to a girl named Momo Sutton, whose right arm ended below the elbow. LaChappelle had been designing prosthetic arms since he was 14. He wanted to change the industry by developing an inexpensive prosthetic body part. Creating Sutton's arm was the fulfillment of his dream. His achievement shows how young entrepreneurs use science and **technology** to develop businesses that can change the world.

ENTREPRENEURS AND START-UPS

An entrepreneur is someone who plans, starts, and runs a new business that provides **goods** or **services**. Entrepreneurs are people who have an original or **innovative** idea, then turn that idea into a business to supply those goods or services. Start-ups are brand-new businesses created by entrepreneurs.

ENTREPRENEURS CHANGING THE WORLD

The medical field is **evolving** at a fast pace. New technologies are changing the way doctors treat disease and are making life easier for people. They are also increasing the number of people who survive illness and injury. But doctors and scientists are also facing challenges, such as how to shorten recovery time or make someone's life as comfortable as possible. Many bright young engineers are meeting these challenges by using their science and technology skills to think creatively, solve problems, and work together.

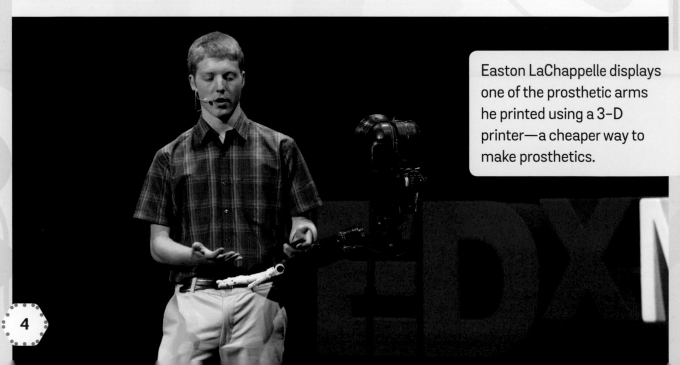

Easton LaChappelle displays one of the prosthetic arms he printed using a 3-D printer—a cheaper way to make prosthetics.

ENTREPRENEURS OF THE FUTURE

Entrepreneurs such as LaChappelle and Emil von Behring (see below) continue to change the world by bringing innovative and important medical products and services to people around the world. You can join them by developing your abilities to think critically, solve problems, be creative, and work with others. These skills will help prepare you for the future, no matter what job you choose!

You can be a medical entrepreneur, too! Start now by taking courses in science, technology, and mathematics.

INSPIRING STORIES

Early Thinkers

Emil von Behring was a doctor who developed the first effective **immunization** against a disease called diphtheria. Von Behring used blood from infected sheep and horses to develop a serum, or liquid, to cure diphtheria.

After experimenting on animals, von Behring treated a child in 1891. He then teamed up with the Hoechst pharmaceutical company to produce and sell the serum. By 1913, von Behring had developed a **vaccine** against diphtheria.

Emil von Behring was born in Prussia (now part of Poland) in 1854.

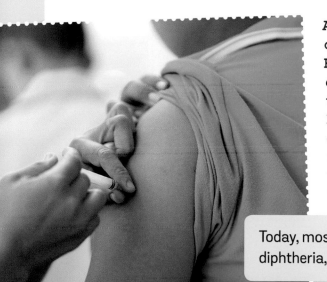

Today, most children are vaccinated against diphtheria, which saves many lives.

SEARCHING FOR A CURE

According to the World Health Organization (WHO), cancer is one of the leading causes of death worldwide. In 2017 in the United States, there were an estimated 1,688,780 new cases of cancer. Many companies work to create and sell treatments for cancer.

FINDING A CURE

Much of that work is done by science entrepreneurs working for enormous companies that make and sell drugs. The cost is high. It can cost $4.2 billion or more to invent, develop, and test a new cancer drug. This is far too much for most start-up companies to afford.

Researchers are working on ways to program the body's natural immune system to attack and kill cancerous tumor cells.

Many treatment advances have been made by international teams of researchers. In 2016, cancer **immunotherapy** became available to people. This uses a patient's own **white blood cells** to help combat their cancer. White blood cells include types of cells called **T-cells**. These cells fight off disease. Researchers continue to work on ways to remove these T-cells and reprogram, or change, them to attack and kill cancerous tumor cells. These new T-cells could kill existing cancer cells and stop them from returning.

EXCITING START-UPS

Some successful cancer start-ups focus on helping prevent cancer. Other companies create products that can assist people who are dealing with the side effects of cancer treatment. In 2012, entrepreneur Lara Little watched her sister suffer night sweats as a result of her breast cancer treatments. The problem gave Lara an idea. Top athletes wear outfits made from material that wicks, or takes, away sweat. Why not develop a line of fashionable pajamas made from the same material?

Little contacted a textile mill in Asia to develop the fabric she needed, and found a factory to manufacture the pajamas. She also hired someone to help her perfect the design, making them attractive and comfortable. The result is Lusomé—a business that tripled its 2015 sales in 2016, and expects to do the same in 2017. "We are headed to a $200-million company," Little says.

Safer Swimming

California actress and entrepreneur Sarah Buxton used science and technology skills to develop tutu*blue*—a full-body swimsuit. This colorful bathing wear is made from material that protects the wearer from the Sun's damaging rays, which can cause skin cancer. The start-up's designs were featured in a February 2016 episode of the television program *Shark Tank*. Since the episode, many people have bought Buxton's swimsuits.

Sarah Buxton's designs not only look great, but they also block the damaging rays of the Sun.

RESEARCH
START-UP STAR:
YEHIA ABUGABAL

In Egypt, about 113,000 cases of cancer are diagnosed each year. Yehia Abugabal is using his entrepreneurial skills to help more people survive the disease. He founded the International Cancer Research Center (ICRC) in Cairo and has been its **CEO** since 2014.

Abugabal always wanted to be a doctor, just like his parents. He went to medical school and became an **oncologist**. Immediately after graduation, he founded the ICRC to research and treat cancer. Abugabal and a top-notch team of doctors and scientists work together to find the causes of specific cancers. They are also working to treat cancer and to find a cure. One of Abugabal's dreams is to increase cancer survival in Egypt. But, to do that successfully, he has to change people's attitudes first.

Cancer cells can quickly multiply in the human body, causing serious problems.

Yehia Abugabal is also CEO of a nonprofit organization that aims to improve care for cancer patients.

ATTITUDE IS KEY

In Egypt, cultural norms can make it difficult for women to get breast cancer diagnosed. Early detection of breast cancer is important to a woman's survival, but many Egyptian women do not know the importance of regular checkups. Some are scared that if they do get a checkup, they might be diagnosed with a serious disease such as cancer. As a result, many women die without ever being diagnosed. Abugabal knows this could be avoided. He believes that young people are the key to changing attitudes. The ICRC is working on a game and a mobile app to teach children about cancer awareness. As the children learn, many will pass on information to their parents.

THE IMPORTANCE OF RESEARCH

Abugabal says a lack of detailed records on cancer patients is a major problem in Egypt. Records give information about patients, their disease, and other details such as where they live. When Abugabal started the ICRC, he and his team created a program to train researchers to analyze records. Once the researchers identify where cancer is most common, they can try to find out what is causing it. For example, records show that there is a high rate of lung cancer in two sections of Cairo. This may be due to pollution. Researchers will try to identify the cancer–causing **pollutant** and find ways to reduce it.

BUILDING RELATIONSHIPS

Abugabal contacted the National Institute of Health (NIH) in the United States. The organization has an excellent training program for their researchers. Abugabal was able to arrange for the NIH to offer its courses to his research staff in Egypt, as well. Abugabal and his staff will continue to work on public awareness, treating patients, and finding a cure for cancer.

The haze in this photo of Cairo suggests the presence of **air pollution**—a possible cause for the area's high lung cancer rates.

HELPING ATHLETES

Today's sports medicine start-ups do more than treat athletes' injuries. They also provide coaching in injury prevention and fitness training. Scientists and technology experts work together to create innovative treatments and injury prevention techniques. These keep athletes on the field—and get them back on the field faster after an injury.

IMPROVED TREATMENT

Doctors have many useful tools for analyzing injuries. For example, they can use an **MRI** to examine the problem area and identify the exact location and extent of any injury. They can also use a procedure known as **arthroscopy**. During arthroscopy, they insert a tiny camera into a joint. This allows them to view—and sometimes repair—the damaged area. Robotic technology takes three-dimensional **CT scans** of injured joints. Surgeons use these images to plan procedures. The plans guide the surgeons and their robot "assistants" as they operate.

CONDITIONING

Start-ups such as CoachMePlus specialize in getting athletes fit and keeping them that way. Launched in 2012, this company based in Buffalo, New York, is run by cofounder Kevin Dawidowicz. Its system includes an interactive workout program and athlete management page. The page tracks each player's height, weight, and other measurements.

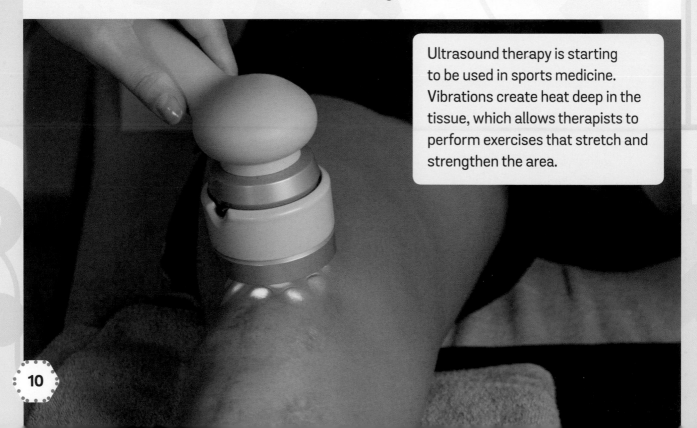

Ultrasound therapy is starting to be used in sports medicine. Vibrations create heat deep in the tissue, which allows therapists to perform exercises that stretch and strengthen the area.

Professional coaches use the program to check whether a team member is following through on training and diet plans. By 2017, one-third of North America's professional sports teams were using CoachMePlus. That year, it expanded to high school and fitness gym athletes.

INJURY PREVENTION

High-speed video provides athletes with information about their body's motion. By analyzing the mechanics, or body movements, of a jump, throw, or swing, experts can predict where injuries might occur and how to prevent many of them.

Since 2014, BodiTrak Sports has built portable mats for golfers to use while practicing their swings. Sensors track a golfer's foot movements, and data goes to a smartphone or desktop app. Golfers can use these to improve the positioning of their feet, legs, and waist to avoid injuries. Within two years, the start-up reported 1,000 customers in 20 countries.

COACHMEPLUS

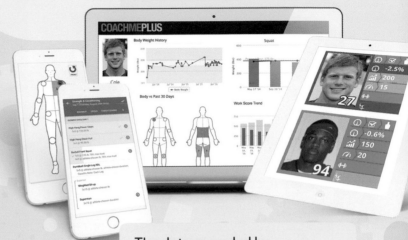

The data recorded by CoachMePlus can be accessed through a smartphone or tablet.

INSPIRING STORIES

Preventing Concussions

Concussions are head injuries that often go unnoticed. But multiple concussions can lead to severe issues with the way a person's brain works. The Concussion Legacy Foundation started a program to increase awareness of this problem. The program helps athletes recognize the signs of concussions so they are not unnoticed. It also helps athletes avoid concussions and seek treatment when they have one. In 2016, the foundation's "Team Up Speak Up" Day reached more than three million athletes.

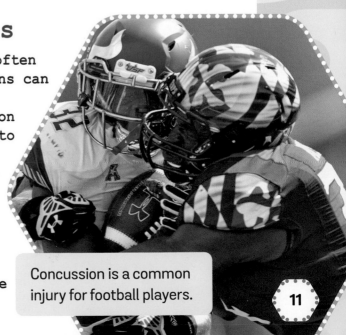

Concussion is a common injury for football players.

PREVENTION
START-UP STAR:
PHIL WAGNER

In California, a medical tech start-up called Sparta Science is helping athletes improve their fitness and reduce injuries. Its founder and CEO, Phil Wagner, is a former strength-and-conditioning coach. When he was studying at the University of Southern California, he learned about force plates. These are used to collect data about athletes while they train. Force plates sense the pressure made by someone standing on them. They create data based on the pressure, which can be used to analyze a person's balance or the way they walk. In 2009, Wagner got a loan with help from the California Small Business Association, and opened Sparta Science to advance the science of force plates.

After working as a conditioning coach, Phil Wagner trained as a doctor before starting Sparta Science.

In 2017, Sparta Science helped the Atlanta Falcons (seen here in training) reach the Super Bowl.

The San Jose Earthquakes have benefited from Sparta Science's injury prevention techniques.

HOW IT WORKS

Wagner came up with an effective way to analyze data from force plates. For Sparta's analysis, athletes perform six vertical jumps in 90 seconds on a square metal plate. Sensors below the plate collect data and feed it into computer software. The results of the best three jumps are shown. The data notes things such as how much force the athlete used to jump. It also notes whether the jump was balanced between the left and right feet.

This data is added to the individual's gender, age, sport, position, injury history, sleep patterns, and **ethnicity**. The results are compared to a large database of other athletes. The system then provides information about any injury the athlete might be at risk for. It also gives suggested workouts to avoid that injury. Athletes receive a list of training suggestions on their cell phone.

PROVEN RESULTS

Results over more than seven years prove the effectiveness of the start-up's technique. The San Jose Earthquakes soccer team started using Sparta Science in 2016. By the second half of that season, the athletes had a 50-percent drop in days missed due to injuries. By the end of the season, soft tissue, such as muscle, injuries had dropped by 80 percent. Other teams have experienced similar improvements, and a resulting drop in medical insurance costs.

These successes helped Wagner raise $2.7 million in 2016. He hired engineers to help organize company data for future analyses. By 2017, the start-up's 15 staff members were serving more than 40 major professional teams and top college teams.

BIONIC PROSTHETICS

Thanks to improvements in technology, today's **bionic** limbs are incredibly advanced. Dean Kamen and his company, DEKA Research & Development, have developed a prosthetic arm called LUKE, which is controlled electronically. **Electrodes** attached to the wearer's arm or shoulder detect, or notice, muscle movement in a person's limb. The electrodes send movement signals to the prosthetic arm, which then interprets the data and moves. The arm can also be controlled by sensors worn on the wearer's shoes. By tilting their feet, the wearer can control the arm's movements and the hand's grip.

In tests, LUKE outperformed older prostheses. It allowed the wearer to pick up objects as small as a grape. Wearers can also pick up and move delicate objects, such as eggs, without breaking them. By mid–2017, more than 100 American citizens, including many **veterans**, had been trained to use LUKE.

BIONIC LEG

In 2017, the **Rehabilitation** Institute of Chicago, designers at Vanderbilt University, and the company Freedom Innovations continued work on a bionic leg. They are using lightweight **graphite** and **microelectronics**. These materials help to improve the leg's ability to move and balance the body without adding weight.

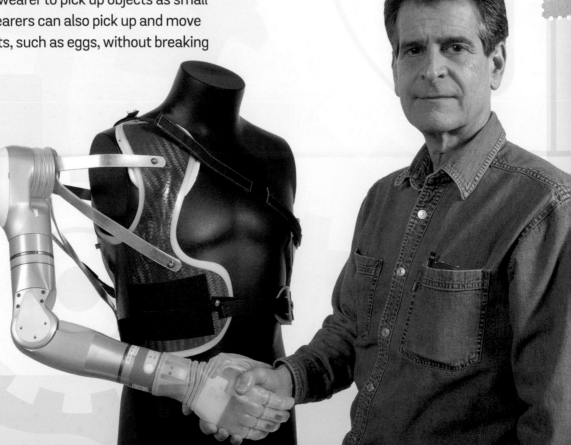

Electrodes from Dean Kamen's LUKE prosthetic arm pick up signals from the wearer's body.

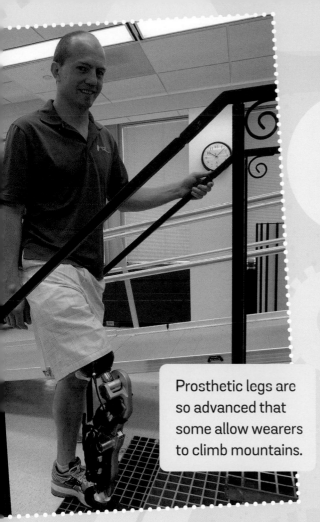

Prosthetic legs are so advanced that some allow wearers to climb mountains.

SMART SKIN

Imagine a prosthetic limb that has artificial skin capable of feeling! In 2014, South Korean researchers developed an artificial "smart" skin. It can detect temperature, humidity, and texture. In 2017, University of Glasgow engineers manufactured a similar skin from **graphene**. The skin is sensitive to touch and is powered by solar energy. With developments like these, it will not be long before science and technology entrepreneurs develop even more life-like prostheses.

START-UP FUNDING

Crowdfunding sites provide start-up funds for many young entrepreneurs. Entrepreneurs describe their project and explain their goals. They use sites such as GoFundMe, Kickstarter, or Indiegogo. People interested in an idea can send donations. Entrepreneurs can also use the sites to see how much interest there is in their ideas.

INSPIRING STORIES

Printing Hands

The big news is printing prosthetics in 3-D. In 2016, medical student Aadeel Akhtar won $18,000 for his work on an inexpensive prosthetic hand. Akhtar worked with mechanical engineering student Patrick Slade. They cofounded Psyonic to develop inexpensive prosthetic hands. At $550, their latest **prototype** is something patients can afford. It takes 30 hours to print on a 3-D printer, and another two hours to assemble. The start-up continues to work on and improve the design.

Patrick Slade (left) and Aadeel Akhtar (right) show off the prosthetic hand they printed on a 3-D printer.

BIONIC
START-UP STAR:
EASTON LACHAPPELLE

In 2010, when he was 14, Easton LaChappelle taught himself about robotics. He used online forums and tutorials to learn everything he could about sensors, motors, and coding. He then built his first robotic hand using plastic building bricks, fishing line, and **surgical tubing**. The result won him third place at the Colorado Science Fair.

While he was at the fair, he met a young girl who was born without an arm. All her prosthetic hand could do was open and close. LaChappelle learned that she would have to get new arms as she grew, and that each one could cost $80,000 or more. He vowed to create something to help people like her.

Easton LaChappelle has tried many different versions of his 3-D-printed prosthetic arm.

The prosthetic arms are designed to use affordable materials and parts.

MODIFYING THE DESIGN

LaChappelle used computer-modeling software to create his second hand, which had humanlike fingers with several joints and a thumb that could bend inward. Small electronic motors in the wrist could curl the fingers. To control the hand, LaChappelle used a 1980s Nintendo Power Glove. Electrodes attached to the wearer's head picked up and read signals from the brain. These were then sent to a special electronic sensor on the arm.

Next, LaChappelle studied 3-D printing and learned how to print an arm for less than $400. In 2013, he founded Unlimited Tomorrow. This start-up makes cutting-edge prosthetics available at little or no cost.

By 2017, LaChappelle had worked through several arm prototypes. That year, he moved his company from his bedroom to a 3,500-square-foot (1,067-square-meter) facility. He also delivered his most recent design to a 10-year-old girl named Momo Sutton.

SUTTONS'S NEW ARM

LaChappelle had someone make a 3-D scan of Sutton's whole left arm with an ordinary webcam. That helped him design a prosthetic the same shape and dimensions as Sutton's original arm. He then printed the design.

To attach the arm to Sutton's limb, he printed 3-D supports that look like a brace. Velcro straps hold it in place. Three electrodes extend from the top and attach to the muscles in Sutton's upper arm to read the muscles' signals and know where to move. A small button on the arm can also act as a muscle. Press once and the index finger moves toward the thumb. Press again and all the fingers curl toward the palm.

LaChappelle used the sensors in a Nintendo Power Glove to help him convert real hand movements into robotic movements that could be done by his prosthesis.

STEM CELL CURES

Biotech companies use modern research and methods to develop cures for diseases that were once incurable. Today, many **biotech** entrepreneurs focus on **stem cells**. Cells are the smallest parts that make up living things. The human body has many different types of cells. These include muscle, skin, blood, bone, and brain cells. However, stem cells are unique. They can become any type of cell the body needs.

Researchers are trying to figure out how to program these cells to turn into a specific type of cell. For example, a stem cell could become a spinal cell to replace a defective, worn-out, or injured spinal cell. But that is still in the future. Today, researchers are studying how to put stem cells to work to heal human conditions. Originally, the stem cells they used came from mice and other animals. As of 1998, they began to work with stem cells taken from **embryos**.

Many laboratories around the world are researching ways to use stem cells to treat diseases.

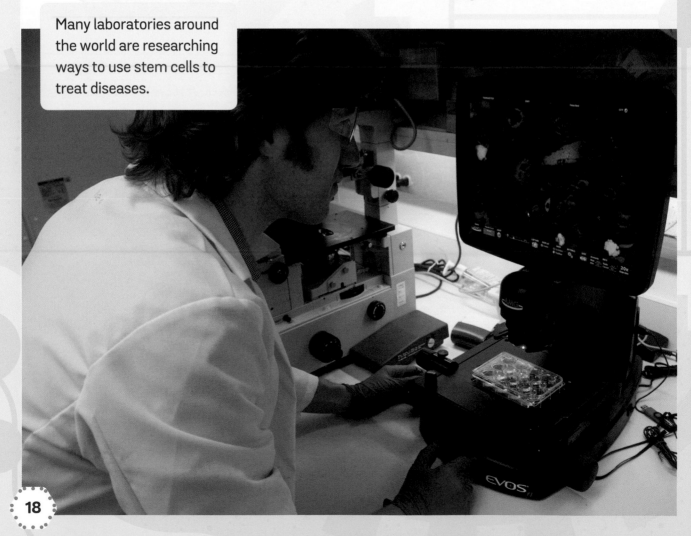

In 2006, researchers discovered that adults could donate stem cells for research. Tissue from an adult's brain, **bone marrow**, blood vessels, skeletal muscle, skin, and liver also contain stem cells. How can these adult stem cells be used to treat and cure diseases and conditions? Entrepreneurs continue to work to find this out.

TODAY'S CURES

Doctors now **transplant** blood stem cells into patients with life-threatening blood cancers such as leukemia. This cure has saved thousands of children. Stem cells are also used to treat bone, skin, and eye conditions.

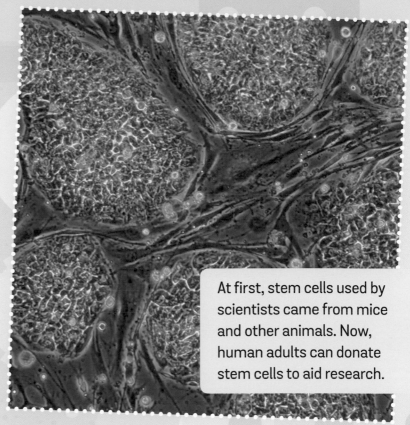

At first, stem cells used by scientists came from mice and other animals. Now, human adults can donate stem cells to aid research.

Doctors are working on ways to use stem cells to grow healthy heart muscle for people with heart disease. They want to replace the damaged brain cells in patients with **Parkinson's disease**. Doctors also believe it will be possible to grow healthy skin for burn victims. A lot of this research is being funded by gigantic biotech labs and facilities. The future potential provides opportunities for stem cell entrepreneurs and their start-ups.

Freeze for the Future

Laura Vaughan is a cofounder of the start-up company Acorn Cryotech. This company collects and preserves clients' stem cells. Clients receive a take-home kit, which they use to collect cells they then send to the company. The cells are cooled to very low temperatures and kept in a deep freeze for later use. They will be available in the future if the owner ever needs them. Before long, it will likely be common to deep freeze the blood from the **umbilical cord** of all newborns. This blood contains potentially life-saving stem cells.

HEART
START-UP STAR:
DIVYA NAG

Heart disease takes 630,000 American lives and costs the country $200 billion each year. To help prevent this, Divya Nag and Andrew Lee started Stem Cell Theranostics in 2011, when Nag was just 20 years old. The term "theranostics" combines the words "therapy" and "diagnostics." It refers to testing patients for possible reactions to a particular drug, then to tailoring a treatment specifically to them.

BEATING CELLS

Nag and her team built on the work of researcher Shinya Yamanaka. He discovered the four **genes** that allow stem cells to turn into regular body cells. Nag and Lee used these genes to transform skin cells into heart cells. "The coolest thing about these heart cells is they actually beat on the dish," she says.

The entrepreneur looks forward to the day when she can inject cells like these into a damaged heart to repair it. The treatment would be a lot easier and less expensive than doing a heart transplant. For now, Theranostics is focusing on using the cells to test new drugs and therapies.

Usually, when companies develop a new drug, they spend five to six years testing it on mice, rats, and hamsters. Theranostics can simplify this process by testing a drug directly on related cells. This method can greatly reduce the time and money it takes to develop a new heart medication. Using this technology, it took Stem Cell Theranostics just two years to develop its treatment ideas.

Testing new drugs and treatments can be a long and costly process.

HELPING OTHER START-UPS

Like many entrepreneurs, Nag is full of ideas. At a young age, she figured out a strategy for young women to break into the male-dominated field of science—by bringing male cofounders along to meetings. Now, to help others, she has started StartX Med. This is a nonprofit entrepreneurship program. The idea is to coach current and former Stanford University students as they develop medical start-ups.

In 2014, Nag accepted a job with Apple. There, she led the team that launched ResearchKit in 2015. This package allows health researchers to create apps that make it easy to share what they are learning. Within its first six months, ResearchKit had attracted 100,000 people to participate in various studies. In June 2017, an update allowed researchers to add video content to their apps.

Shinya Yamanaka (second from left) won a Nobel Prize for his work on stem cells.

24-HOUR MEDICINE

Today, people can carry or wear items that improve their health. Wearable medical pumps deliver such things as painkillers or **insulin**. Users can set smartphones to give medication reminders, manage **diabetes**, and access lab results. The Apple Watch's heart-rate sensor can detect a condition called **arrhythmia**, in which a person's heartbeat is irregular. Products such as Fitbit measure the number of steps walked, heart rate, and quality of sleep.

But the big news is smart clothing. You can wear shirts that monitor your heart rate, breathing, and movement. Bathing suits warn when you have had enough sun. There is a growing demand for smart clothing, so many young entrepreneurs are innovating in this area.

FROM STROKE TO START-UP

In 2009, Dustin Freckleton was 24 and a medical student at the University of Texas–Houston when he suffered a stroke caused by **dehydration**. He recovered, and by 2013, he had completed both a medical degree and a business degree. He was determined to prevent similar strokes in other people.

Using $1.2 million raised through Kickstarter, Freckleton put together a team that developed the LVL Hydration Monitor. The start-up's device uses **infrared light** to measure the amount of water in the wearer's blood. It warns when they need a drink of water. It also tracks heart rate, activity level, number of calories burned, and sleep patterns. By 2017, Freckleton was taking orders for his new device.

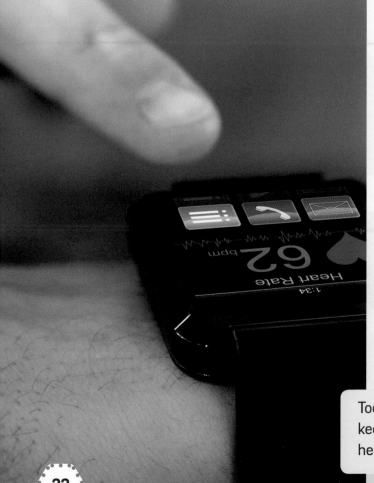

Today, a smart watch can keep track of the wearer's heart rate.

WEARABLE TECHNOLOGY

Wearable devices will soon transmit health information directly to doctors. A device called Bodytrak uses an in-ear device to track a person's core temperature, heart rate, oxygen volume, and other health data. In early 2017, its inventors started clinical trials at a hospital in London, England. In the future, Bodytrak may track the health of post-surgery patients and those with chronic conditions.

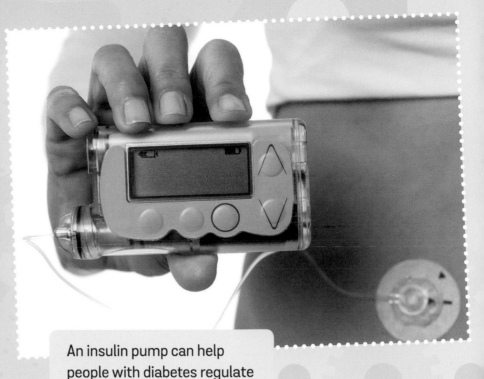

An insulin pump can help people with diabetes regulate their blood sugar.

INSPIRING STORIES

Smart Diapers

In 2012, Yaroslav Faybishenko realized that the urine in his child's diaper could provide a warning about possible health problems. A person's urine can indicate different diseases and also dehydration. Faybishenko and his wife, Jennie Rubinshteyn, founded Pixie Scientific. With funding raised on Indiegogo, they developed what they call "smart diapers." These diapers have a panel that changes color when it detects something unhealthy or unusual in a baby's urine. The couple's product has morphed into Pixie Pads, a similar product for senior citizens in nursing homes.

A baby cannot tell her parents when something is wrong, but the urine in her diaper could provide clues.

BABY MONITOR
START-UP STARS:
SONA SHAH AND TERESA CAUVEL

It is a sad fact that every year, nearly three million babies around the world die during their first month of life. But more babies in Uganda will survive and thrive thanks to Sona Shah and Teresa Cauvel. These two entrepreneurs have fitted monitors into wearable bands worn by newborn babies.

EARLY SUCCESS

The pair first teamed up in 2015. They were both working on their master's degree in biomedical engineering at Columbia University. They visited Uganda and learned that 19 out of every 1,000 newborns in the country died. Shah and Cauvel decided to find a way to save more babies. In 2015, a **business accelerator** provided the money and **mentorship** they needed. Shah and Cauvel developed a business plan for their start-up, Neopenda. They built and tested several prototypes for their product. It is a device that monitors a baby's vital signs.

In 2016, they won $300,000 from the Vodafone Americas Foundation's Wireless Innovation Project. They also received nearly $150,000 from other sources, including a Kickstarter campaign.

Sona Shah (left) and Teresa Cauvel (right) run Neopenda from Chicago. Their business saves the lives of babies in Uganda.

24

SMART BABY MONITORS

Shah and Cauvel completed a prototype, filed for a **patent**, and hired a coordinator in Uganda to help with a **field study**. By 2017, their devices were back in Uganda to get feedback from nurses and to start testing. Some hospitals in Uganda may have only one nurse to care for 150 babies. With so few staff and so many patients, a child may die before anyone even knows he or she is in trouble.

Neopenda's affordable monitors are reusable, making them cost-effective. Each monitor detects the wearer's temperature, heart rate, breathing rate, and level of oxygen in the blood. Data is wirelessly delivered to a tablet. Nurses can monitor the information and provide treatment when needed. The system was developed to allow one nurse to monitor up to 24 babies at a glance. The nurse can check one screen, then quickly see how the babies on another screen are doing. This allows a small number of nurses to care for a larger number of babies.

The plastic case on this prototype was printed on a 3-D printer. It holds the sensors used to monitor babies.

SAVING LIVES

In Uganda, Neopenda works with hospitals, doctors, and public health officials. Shah and Cauvel teach local engineers about their device, and continue to make improvements. In March 2017, they were finalists for the World Changing Ideas Awards. That year, they also won a grant from the IEEE Special Interest Group on Humanitarian Technology. By working on innovative solutions to urgent health challenges, Neopenda strives to give newborns in Uganda the shot at a healthy start to life that they deserve.

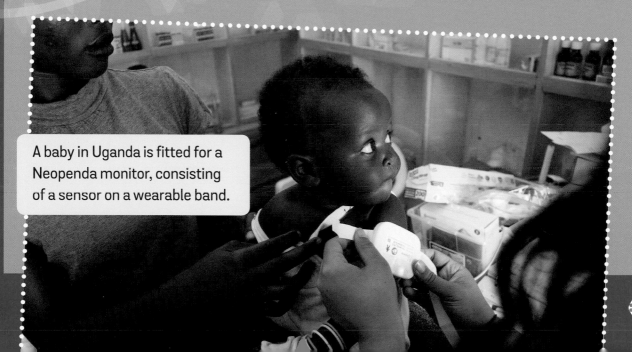

A baby in Uganda is fitted for a Neopenda monitor, consisting of a sensor on a wearable band.

ENTREPRENEURS CHANGING THE WORLD

During the past 100 years, science and technology entrepreneurs have made incredible advances. These advances have increased the life expectancy of Americans from about 46 years for men and 48 years for women in 1900, to 76 years for men and 81 for women in 2017. Science and technology advances continue to lead the way in preventing and treating medical conditions.

ARTIFICIAL INTELLIGENCE

A Hungarian company called Turbine is using **artificial intelligence** to map out and imitate cancer cells on a computer. The 2015 start-up combines a knowledge of technology and biology to compare healthy cells to cancerous cells. Its programs predict which therapies the cells may resist. This guides treatment options. Turbine hopes to assist drug companies in choosing the best combination of new and old treatments for specific cancer types.

Turbine can map out brain cancer cells, like this one, to see how they behave.

The blue areas show the places that have been properly disinfected using Highlight. The blue color will disappear after a short period of time.

DETECTING PATHOGENS

The start-up PathVis has spent five years developing a method of using a smartphone to detect tiny living things that can cause disease. Usually, if people suspect that a water source is infected by **cholera**, they take a sample and send it to the lab. Meanwhile, people drink the water and could get sick. The PathVis device can detect the presence of cholera **pathogens** within 30 minutes.

It is "like a portable laboratory," says cofounder and CEO Katherine Clayton, who worked with a team to develop the app. The start-up is working to expand the capability of its device. Soon it may be able to detect such diseases as malaria and HIV.

Another company, Kinnos, has a low-tech solution for killing pathogens. Its product is a substance called Highlight that can be added to a disinfectant. The mixture turns blue when it is sprayed, which shows health-care workers what areas have been sterilized. Lack of color means an area still needs to be cleaned. When the blue color fades away, it means that the decontamination is finished. According to cofounders Jason Kang, Katherine Jin, and Kevin Tyan, their product has the potential to protect workers and the public from deadly infections that are passed around easily in a hospital setting.

YOUR START-UP STORY

Entrepreneurs continue to make huge strides in producing new medical devices and treatments. They are finding new ways to diagnose and treat many conditions. They are developing tools that make it easier to live with life-changing injuries. You can be one of these entrepreneurs.

TAKE THE START-UP CHALLENGE!

Although you may not be ready to start work on a prosthetic hand, there are problems you can help to solve now. Every year, emergency crews pick up injured people. It may be an elderly person who has slipped on the ice and become unconscious. It may be a toddler who has wandered away from her caretaker and got hit by a car. Or it may be a pre-teen who fell climbing a soccer net.

Sometimes, medical teams cannot find identification on a person, and have no knowledge of their medical history. It is harder for them to treat patients when they do not know their age and weight, any allergies, and whether they have any existing health problems. There may be a need for a product that people can always keep with them to help medical staff in an emergency. Solving this problem could provide an entrepreneur with a business idea. Perhaps that person will be you!

You may wish to design an electronic device. Or maybe you will go low-tech instead!

START-UP CHALLENGE
DESIGN AN ID DEVICE

First, you need to decide what form your ID device should take. Could it be a card people carry? A piece of jewelry they wear? A computer chip put into the body? Research the types of identification tags currently used, both for humans and for animals. What are the advantages and disadvantages of each system? How can you improve on them? Remember that people of all ages and lifestyles may decide to wear your invention. Will you develop a choice of styles and colors?

Think about what material you will use. Substances that easily break or wear away under rough conditions will not stand up to constant use. Many users will also look for **hypoallergenic** materials.

Do not forget to decide what information the ID should contain. The person's name and contact information for next of kin might help. What else might be included?

Research the type of information medical staff need to know about patients before starting treatment. Interview someone who wears a MedicAlert bracelet. Find out what types of information these bracelets include, and why. Talk to people with life–threatening conditions such as severe allergies. What information do medical staff need before treating them?

Keep asking questions and adding to your findings. Who knows, perhaps you might come up with a brilliant entrepreneurial idea that could change the world!

In an emergency, knowing a patient's medical history could mean the difference between life and death.

GLOSSARY

3-D printer A printer that makes solid objects from a file of digital instructions

air pollution Presence in the air of a substance that is harmful or poisonous

arrhythmia Condition in which the heart beats with an irregular or abnormal rhythm

arthroscopy A procedure for diagnosing and treating joint problems

artificial intelligence Computer software that can perform tasks usually done by humans

bionic Refers to artificial body parts that are usually electromechanical

biotech Short form for biotechnology; refers to the use of biology and technology to develop a medical treatment or cure

bone marrow A soft, fatty substance inside bones, in which new blood cells are made

business accelerator Company that provides support and funding opportunities for start-ups

CEO (short for **Chief Executive Officer**) A person who is in charge of a company

cholera Serious infection caused by bacteria and often spread in contaminated water

concussions Temporary unconsciousness caused by a blow to the head; also refers to the after-effects of such a blow

CT scans Computerized scans that create a 3-D view from a series of X-ray images

dehydration Loss of water

diabetes Condition in which the pancreas does not make enough insulin to regulate the amount of sugar in a person's blood

electrodes Electrical sensors

embryos Unborn or unhatched offspring at the beginning stages of development

entrepreneur A person who creates a business and takes on most of the risk to operate it

ethnicity Refers to belonging to a social group that has a common cultural tradition

evolving Changing over time

field study Collecting data outside a lab or experimental setting

genes Units of heredity passed on from a parent that determine the offspring's traits

goods Products; something made

graphene A form of lightweight carbon

graphite Gray form of carbon found in some rocks, often used in the core of pencils

hypoallergenic Unlikely to cause an allergic reaction

immunization Injection of a small amount of a disease to make someone immune to it

immunotherapy Prevention or treatment of disease by stimulating the body's natural immune response

infrared light Light that has a wavelength between visible light and microwaves

innovative Describing something that no one else has done before

insulin A natural hormone produced in the pancreas that regulates the amount of sugar in the blood

mentorship Guidance provided by a mentor or coach

microelectronics The design, manufacture, and use of tiny microchips and microcircuits

MRI Magnetic resonance imaging; using large magnets to produce clear images of the body's internal organs

oncologist Doctor who specializes in treating cancer patients

Parkinson's disease Progressive condition of the nervous system that causes tremors, rigid muscles, and slow movement

patent A government license for ownership of an invention

pathogens Bacteria, viruses, or other microorganisms that can cause disease

pollutant Substance that contaminates the water or air

prosthetic Artificial limb

prototype Early model of an invention that is used for testing

rehabilitation Restoring someone to health through training and therapy

services Types of help or work that someone does for someone else

stem cells Unique body cells that can become any type of body cell

surgical tubing Piece of rubber tube used to connect pieces of apparatus or for drainage during medical procedures

T-cells A type of cell involved in the body's immune response

technology Using science to develop practical solutions to problems

transplant Move or transfer a body part from one body to another, such as replacing a patient's defective organ with a donated organ from someone else

umbilical cord The flexible cord that attaches a mammal to its fetus during early development inside the mother

vaccine Inoculation used to encourage the body to develop immunity against a specific disease

veterans People who have fought as soldiers in a war

white blood cells A type of blood cell the body makes to help fight infection

LEARNING MORE

BOOKS

Bryant, Jill. *Medical Inventions: The Best of Health.* Crabtree Publishing Company, 2013.

Carmichael, L.E. *Innovations in Health.* Crabtree Publishing Company, 2017.

Eamer, Claire. *Before the World Was Ready.* Annick Press, 2013.

Sutherland, Adam. *Be a Young Entrepreneur.* Barron's Educational Series, 2016.

Williams, Gabrielle J. *The Making of a Young Entrepreneur: A Kid's Guide to Developing the Mind-Set for Success.* Legacy Builder Group, LLC, 2011.

WEBSITES

Arduino Animatronic Hand
www.sparkfun.com/news/580
When he was 15, Easton LaChappelle explained how his original hand worked.

TEDFellows
https://fellowsblog.ted.com/7-innovations-that-will-change-the-future-of-medicine-62e1b50ad623
Learn about seven innovations that will change the future of medicine.

TEDTalks
www.ted.com/talks/eva_vertes_looks_to_the_future_of_medicine
Learn about the future of cancer research.

WatchKnowLearn
www.watchknowlearn.org/Video.aspx?VideoID=37064&CategoryID=4970 Learn how a sea worm's natural glue could help heal broken bones.

INDEX

ABOUT THE AUTHOR

Helen Mason was diagnosed with Hodgkin's disease in 1968. Thanks to medical research, she was among the first group of patients cured of this cancer of the lymphatic system. She was also part of a long-term study to help with the treatment of other patients. This is her 35th book.